AF425276

FINTECH REVOLUTION IN INDIA

OPPORTUNITIES AND CHALLENGES

CA DR. BRAJESH KUMAR JAISWAL

Copyright © CA Dr. Brajesh Kumar Jaiswal
All Rights Reserved.

This book has been self-published with all reasonable efforts taken to make the material error-free by the author. No part of this book shall be used, reproduced in any manner whatsoever without written permission from the author, except in the case of brief quotations embodied in critical articles and reviews.

The Author of this book is solely responsible and liable for its content including but not limited to the views, representations, descriptions, statements, information, opinions and references ["Content"]. The Content of this book shall not constitute or be construed or deemed to reflect the opinion or expression of the Publisher or Editor. Neither the Publisher nor Editor endorse or approve the Content of this book or guarantee the reliability, accuracy or completeness of the Content published herein and do not make any representations or warranties of any kind, express or implied, including but not limited to the implied warranties of merchantability, fitness for a particular purpose. The Publisher and Editor shall not be liable whatsoever for any errors, omissions, whether such errors or omissions result from negligence, accident, or any other cause or claims for loss or damages of any kind, including without limitation, indirect or consequential loss or damage arising out of use, inability to use, or about the reliability, accuracy or sufficiency of the information contained in this book.

Made with ♥ on the Notion Press Platform
www.notionpress.com

"Dedicated to the innovative minds and resilient spirits shaping India's future, whose relentless pursuit of progress inspires this exploration of the FinTech Revolution."

୬

Contents

Prayer — vii

About The Author — ix

Preface — xi

1. The Dawn Of FinTech: Tracing The Evolution In India — 1

Part 1

2. Digital Payments: The Heartbeat Of Indian FinTech — 7

Part 2

3. Banking Reimagined: FinTech's Impact On Traditional Banking — 13

Part 3

4. Blockchain Revolution: Beyond Cryptocurrency — 19

Part 4

5. Peer-to-Peer Lending: Democratizing Credit — 27

Part 5

6. Crowdfunding: A New Era Of Investment — 35

Part 6

7. Financial Inclusion: Bridging The Gap With Technology — 41

Part 7

8. Regulatory Landscapes: Navigating Compliance And Innovation — 47

Part 8

9. Cybersecurity In FinTech: Safeguarding The Digital Frontier — 55

Part 9

10. Artificial Intelligence In Finance: The Smart Money — 63

Part 10

11. Mobile Wallets: The Convenience Factor — 71

Contents

Part 11

12. InsurTech: Redefining Insurance In India   77

Part 12

13. WealthTech: Personal Finance Management   83

Part 13

14. Neobanks: The Future Of Banking?"   89

Part 14

15. UPI And Its Transformational Impact   95

Part 15

16. Challenges In Adoption: The Roadblocks To FinTech Success   101

Part 16

17. Financial Literacy And Consumer Education   107

Part 17

18. The Rural Reach: FinTech In India's Countryside   113

Part 18

19. Sustainable FinTech: Aligning With Environmental Goals   119

Part 19

20. Global Comparison: India's FinTech Scene In The World Arena   127

Part 20

21. The Road Ahead: Future Trends And Predictions In Indian FinTech   133

Part 21

Citation And Reference   139

CONTACT   141

PRAYER

"May this book illuminate the paths of those navigating the dynamic waters of India's FinTech landscape. Let it be a beacon for knowledge, understanding, and ethical progress, guiding readers towards a future where technology and tradition harmoniously coexist for the betterment of all."

৪৩

About The Author

CA Brajesh Kumar Jaiswal, a distinguished member of the Institute of Chartered Accountants of India (ICAI) since 1996, has made significant contributions in the field of finance and accounting. Born on October 6, 1968, in India, Brajesh's journey in the world of finance was inspired by his late father, Krishna Chandra Jaiswal. His impressive academic record includes qualifications such as FCA (2001), DISA (ICAI) (2004), and CCFAFP (2015), highlighting his commitment to continuous learning and professional development.

Since 1996, Brajesh has been a senior partner at M/s Jaiswal Brajesh & Co., headquartered in Patna with branches across Varanasi, Lucknow, Allahabad, Ranchi, Raipur, and Delhi. His expertise spans a wide range of financial services, including consultancy in Income Tax, Service Tax, and World Bank assisted projects, as well as Audit Services in various government organizations and Public Sector Units (PSUs). He has an extensive experience in conducting various types of audits such as Statutory Audit, Concurrent Audit, Revenue Audit, and IS Audit, particularly in Public Sector Banks, PSUs, and state PSUs.

Brajesh's area of specialization extends to investment consulting. He has been a Professional Investment Expert member of the Investment Committee at Banaras Hindu University since 2012, offering his expertise in banking and investment activities. His role as an Investment Consultant at IIT BHU Varanasi between 2012 and 2014 further emphasizes his proficiency in this domain. Additionally, he served as the Principal Director for DEAS implementation in Patna Municipal Corporation since December 2016 and is an active member of the Indo American Chamber of Commerce in Uttar Pradesh.

A passionate educator, Brajesh has been a key speaker on GST reforms, sharing his knowledge at various universities and colleges. His engagements include lectures at MGKVP University, Varanasi, Arya Mahila Degree College, Varanasi, DAV Degree College, Varanasi, and Agrasen Mahila PG College.

Brajesh's commitment to his profession is evident through his active participation in the Institute of Chartered Accountants of India, Varanasi (CIRC). He has been elected to various executive roles, including Secretary, Treasurer, Vice Chairman, and Chairman, reflecting his leadership and dedication to the field.

His contributions extend beyond professional realms into social service. He has served as a Co-opted member in various committees of the Central India Regional Council of the ICAI and was a member of the Young Members Innovation Development Committee of ICAI, New Delhi, in 2018-19. Furthermore, Brajesh has been a vocal participant in debates and discussions on important economic topics such as the Budget, GST, and the Indian economy, organized by various print media outlets.

CA Brajesh Kumar Jaiswal's career is a testament to his expertise, leadership, and unwavering commitment to both his profession and community.

PREFACE

Welcome to "FinTech Revolution in India: Opportunities and Challenges", a book that aims to unravel the complex and dynamic world of Financial Technology in India – a country at the cusp of a digital financial metamorphosis.

In this book, I have embarked on a journey to explore the multifaceted landscape of FinTech in India. My motivation stems from a deep fascination with the transformative power of technology in the financial sector and a keen interest in how this revolution is unfolding in one of the world's fastest-growing economies. India's unique socio-economic fabric, coupled with its technological leapfrogging, presents a compelling narrative of innovation, adaptation, and resilience.

The chapters within this book are crafted to offer a comprehensive overview of the Indian FinTech ecosystem. They delve into various aspects of the sector, from the burgeoning growth of digital payments to the emerging challenges of cybersecurity. Each chapter is an attempt to provide insights into how technology is not just reshaping financial services, but also redefining the economic and social contours of India.

As the sole author of this book, my journey in compiling these chapters has been enlightening. It involved extensive research, numerous conversations with industry experts, and an in-depth analysis of the trends and policies shaping FinTech in India. The aim has been to present a balanced view that not only highlights the remarkable opportunities but also candidly discusses the challenges facing the sector.

This book is intended for a wide range of readers – from financial professionals and students to policymakers and enthusiasts of technology and finance. Whether you are deeply involved in the FinTech sector or are merely curious about the digital transformation of financial services in India, this book aims to provide valuable insights and a thorough understanding of the subject.

As we stand at the brink of a financial revolution, it is imperative to understand the forces driving this change and the potential impact it holds. "FinTech Revolution in India: Opportunities and Challenges" is a step in that direction – an endeavor to encapsulate the spirit and substance of FinTech in India.

I hope this book enlightens, informs, and inspires you as much as the journey of writing it has for me.

CA Brajesh Kumar Jaiswal
Varanasi

I

The Dawn of FinTech: Tracing the Evolution in India

Historical Perspective and Evolution of FinTech in India

The story of financial technology, or FinTech, in India, is a narrative of revolution, resilience, and remarkable growth. It's a tale that begins in the late 20th century and evolves into a 21st-century saga of innovation and transformation in the financial services sector.

The Early Years: Setting the Stage

The genesis of FinTech in India can be traced back to the 1990s when the country embarked on a journey of economic liberalization. This era marked the beginning of a new financial landscape with the establishment of private banks and the entry of foreign banks into the Indian market. The Reserve Bank of India (RBI), India's central banking institution, played a pivotal role in laying down the regulatory framework that would later become the bedrock of FinTech evolution.

The Advent of Internet Banking

The late 1990s and early 2000s saw the birth of internet banking in India. Pioneered by major banks like ICICI and HDFC, this was the first instance of digital technology merging with financial services. It paved the way for a more tech-savvy customer base, setting the scene for more advanced FinTech innovations.

The Mobile Revolution

The real catalyst for the FinTech boom was the widespread adoption of mobile technology in the 2010s. India's vast population, coupled with the increasing accessibility of smartphones and affordable data plans, created a fertile ground for mobile-based financial solutions. This period witnessed the emergence of mobile wallets like Paytm and Mobikwik, which revolutionized the way people conducted daily financial transactions.

Demonetization: A Turning Point

A significant milestone in the FinTech journey was the Indian government's demonetization move in 2016, where high-denomination currency notes were suddenly invalidated. This bold step, aimed at curbing corruption and black money, inadvertently gave a massive boost to digital payments. Cash-dependent consumers and businesses rapidly shifted to digital platforms, marking a steep rise in FinTech adoption.

UPI: A Game Changer

The introduction of the Unified Payments Interface (UPI) by the National Payments Corporation of India (NPCI) in 2016 was a game-changer. UPI allowed for instant, real-time transfers between two parties, revolutionizing the peer-to-peer (P2P) payment landscape.

This innovation positioned India at the forefront of digital payment technology globally.

The Role of Government and Regulatory Bodies

Initiatives like 'Digital India' and supportive policies have fostered a conducive environment for FinTech growth. The RBI and other regulatory bodies have played a balancing act, encouraging innovation while ensuring consumer protection and financial stability. For instance, the establishment of a regulatory sandbox allowed FinTech startups to test their products in a controlled environment.

The Surge of Startups and Venture Capital

The 2010s also saw a surge in FinTech startups, driven by a combination of technological advancements, entrepreneurial spirit, and venture capital interest. Cities like Bangalore, Mumbai, and Gurgaon became hubs for FinTech innovation, attracting both talent and investment. These startups covered a broad spectrum of services, from digital payments and lending to personal finance management and insurance.

The Inclusion Impact

One of the most significant impacts of FinTech in India has been financial inclusion. FinTech solutions have reached unbanked and underbanked segments of the population, offering them access to financial services that were previously out of reach. Services like micro-lending, affordable insurance, and digital savings platforms have helped integrate a larger section of the population into the formal financial system.

Looking Back to Look Forward

As we trace the evolution of FinTech in India, it becomes evident that this journey has been about much more than just technology. It's about how innovation has democratized financial services, made them more accessible, and transformed the way Indians interact with money. From its early days of internet banking to the current landscape brimming with diverse FinTech offerings, India's FinTech story is one of rapid growth, resilience in the face of challenges, and an unwavering spirit of innovation.

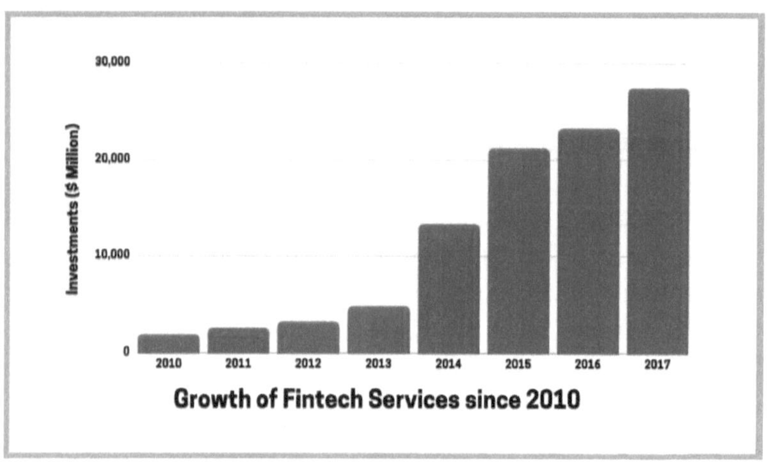

Growth of Fitech Services Since 2010

"In India's FinTech revolution, every digital transaction weaves a new thread in the fabric of economic progress."

৪৩

II

Digital Payments: The Heartbeat of Indian FinTech

In-Depth Look at Digital Payment Systems and Their Growth

In the dynamic landscape of Indian FinTech, digital payments have emerged as the central pillar, driving both innovation and inclusion.

The Genesis and Growth Trajectory

Digital payments in India initially began as an extension of traditional banking services, primarily through online banking portals. However, the landscape took a dramatic turn with the advent of mobile technology and the entry of dedicated payment service providers. The simplicity and convenience offered by these platforms led to their rapid adoption among the urban and later, rural populations.

Mobile Wallets: The Early Innovators

Pioneers like Paytm, Mobikwik, and Freecharge, introduced the concept of mobile wallets in India. These wallets allowed users to store money digitally and make payments for a variety of services. The ease of setting up and using these wallets, along with the added benefits of discounts and cashback offers, appealed to a young, tech-savvy population, setting off the first wave of digital payment adoption.

The Demonetization Boost

The unforeseen event of demonetization in 2016 served as a catalyst for a significant shift from cash to digital payments. With cash in short supply, both consumers and merchants were compelled to adopt digital payment methods. This period saw a meteoric rise in the usage of mobile wallets and the introduction of numerous new players in the market.

UPI: Revolutionizing Peer-to-Peer Transfers

The Unified Payments Interface (UPI) platform, launched by NPCI, revolutionized digital payments by simplifying and securing transactions. UPI allowed users to transfer money across different bank accounts via a single mobile application, using just a virtual payment address. Its interoperability and ease of use led to its widespread acceptance, making it a cornerstone of India's digital payment ecosystem.

The Role of QR Codes

The introduction of QR code-based payments further simplified digital transactions. Small merchants and street vendors, who previously relied solely on cash, started adopting QR codes, thus becoming part of the digital payment revolution. This not only democratized digital payments but also played a critical role in financial inclusion.

Impact of COVID-19 Pandemic

The COVID-19 pandemic and the ensuing social distancing norms gave a further boost to digital payments, as contactless transactions became the norm. The pandemic accelerated the adoption of digital payments across all sections of society, and what was once a convenience, became a necessity.

Challenges and Opportunities

Despite the rapid growth, digital payments in India face challenges such as cybersecurity threats, digital literacy, and reaching remote areas lacking robust internet infrastructure. However, these challenges also present opportunities for innovation and growth in areas like secure payment technologies, offline payment solutions, and financial education initiatives.

The Future Landscape

The future of digital payments in India is poised for further innovation with the integration of technologies like blockchain, artificial intelligence, and the potential advent of Central Bank Digital Currencies (CBDCs). The sector is also likely to see more personalized and value-added services, catering to the diverse needs of a vast and varied user base.

Digital payments have not just been a technological phenomenon but a socio-economic changer in India. They have transformed the way people transact, brought millions into the formal economy, and set the foundation for a more inclusive and efficient financial system. As this chapter concludes, it's evident that digital payments are indeed the heartbeat of the FinTech revolution in India, pulsating with endless possibilities and opportunities.

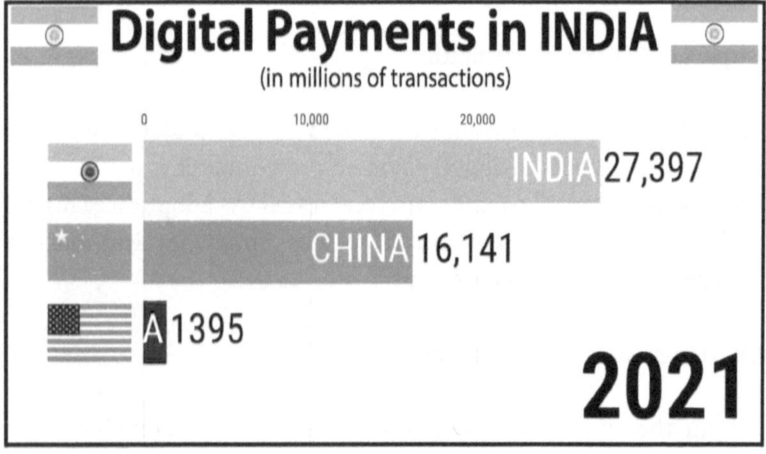

Digital Payments in India

"FinTech in India is not just a sector; it's a gateway to financial inclusion for millions."

౮

III

Banking Reimagined: FinTech's Impact on Traditional Banking

Analysis of How FinTech is Transforming Conventional Banking Models

The advent of FinTech has not only introduced new financial technologies but has also fundamentally altered the traditional banking landscape. This chapter explores how FinTech innovations are reshaping the banking sector in India, presenting both challenges and opportunities for traditional banks.

The Shift to Digital Banking

FinTech's first and most apparent impact has been the acceleration of digital banking. Traditional banks, once reliant on physical branches, are now offering a wide array of services online. Customers can open accounts, apply for loans, and manage investments from their smartphones. This shift has forced banks to rethink their digital strategies and invest in technology to enhance the customer experience.

Enhanced Customer Experience

FinTech innovations have raised customer expectations. Features like real-time payments, 24/7 customer service, personalized financial advice, and user-friendly interfaces are now standard expectations. Traditional banks are responding by adopting FinTech tools like chatbots for customer service, AI for personalized banking advice, and blockchain for secure transactions.

Collaboration and Competition: The FinTech-Bank Relationship

While FinTech firms initially appeared as competitors to traditional banks, a trend of collaboration has emerged. Banks are partnering with FinTech companies to leverage their technological expertise and innovative solutions. This symbiotic relationship enables banks to modernize their operations and FinTech firms to expand their reach.

Impact on Financial Services

FinTech has democratized access to financial services. Features like micro-lending, peer-to-peer lending platforms, and digital-only banks have opened up new avenues for consumers who were previously underserved by traditional banks. This inclusivity is pushing banks to expand their service portfolios and reach out to new customer segments.

The Challenge of Regulatory Compliance

One of the significant challenges for traditional banks in embracing FinTech is navigating the complex web of financial regulations. FinTech startups, with their agility and innovative models, often operate in regulatory grey areas. In contrast, banks are bound by stricter regulatory frameworks, making it challenging to innovate at the same pace.

Cybersecurity Concerns

As banking services move online, cybersecurity becomes a paramount concern. Traditional banks, in adopting FinTech solutions, must also invest heavily in securing digital transactions and safeguarding customer data against the growing threat of cyber-attacks.

Redefining the Banking Workforce

FinTech is also transforming the skillset required in the banking sector. There is a growing need for professionals skilled in data analytics, cybersecurity, and digital marketing. This shift is leading to a retraining of the existing workforce and a change in hiring practices.

FinTech's impact on traditional banking is a story of transformation and adaptation. It's a narrative where technology is not just an enabler but a driver of change, compelling banks to reimagine their operations, customer engagement models, and even their core business philosophies. As traditional banks integrate more FinTech solutions, the line between a bank and a FinTech company continues to blur,

leading to a more innovative, customer-centric, and inclusive banking landscape. This transformation, though challenging, is creating a more dynamic financial ecosystem in India, capable of serving a diverse and rapidly evolving customer base.

The future of banking in India, influenced by the relentless pace of FinTech innovation, promises a more integrated, efficient, and accessible financial system. It's a future where traditional banks and FinTech firms coexist and collaborate, leveraging each other's strengths to redefine the contours of the banking industry. In this reimagined world of banking, the ultimate winners are the consumers, who benefit from enhanced services, better accessibility, and more personalized banking experiences.

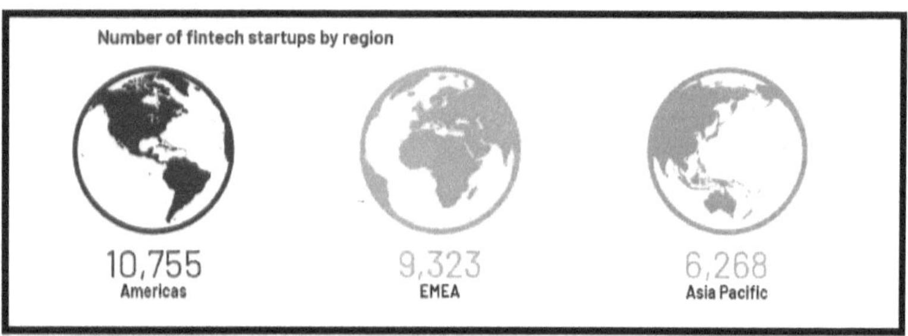

Number of Fintech Startups by Region (Pic Source: acuitykp.com/ blog/fintech-in-banking)

"The beauty of India's FinTech is in turning challenges into stepping stones for innovation."

ॐ

IV
Blockchain Revolution: Beyond Cryptocurrency

Exploring Blockchain Applications in Indian Financial Sectors

The term 'blockchain' is often synonymous with cryptocurrencies, but its applications extend far beyond the realms of digital currency. This chapter delves into the transformative role of blockchain technology in various financial sectors in India, highlighting how it goes beyond just cryptocurrency.

Understanding Blockchain Technology

Before exploring its applications, it's essential to demystify blockchain. It is a decentralized ledger technology (DLT) that records transactions across many computers in a way that the records cannot be altered retroactively. This technology offers transparency, security, and immutability, making it appealing for various applications.

Revolutionizing Banking Operations

Indian banks are exploring blockchain to enhance operational efficiency and security. Blockchain can streamline processes like Know Your Customer (KYC) verification, loan disbursal, and cross-border payments. By creating a decentralized and transparent system, blockchain reduces the risk of fraud, speeds up transactions, and lowers operational costs.

Enhancing Supply Chain Finance

Blockchain can revolutionize supply chain finance by providing a transparent and efficient system for tracking the production, shipment, and receipt of products. It enables all parties in the supply chain to access real-time information, thereby reducing delays, preventing fraud, and improving overall supply chain efficiency.

Improving Government Transactions

The Indian government has shown interest in adopting blockchain for various applications, including land registry, e-governance, and public health. Blockchain can help in creating tamper-proof records, thereby enhancing transparency and reducing corruption in government transactions.

Impact on Insurance Sector

Blockchain has the potential to significantly impact the insurance sector. Smart contracts, which are self-executing contracts with the terms of the agreement directly written into code, can automate claim processing and payouts, reducing fraud, and improving efficiency.

Security Token Offerings (STOs)

Beyond cryptocurrencies, blockchain is being used for Security Token Offerings (STOs) in India. STOs are digital assets backed by real assets like property or stocks. They provide a more secure and regulated investment option compared to traditional cryptocurrencies.

Challenges in Implementation

Despite its potential, blockchain faces challenges in widespread adoption. These include regulatory uncertainty, the need for a robust technological infrastructure, and issues related to scalability and interoperability. The lack of awareness and understanding of blockchain technology also poses a significant challenge.

The Road Ahead

The future of blockchain in India looks promising, with both the public and private sectors exploring its applications. As the technology matures and awareness grows, blockchain

has the potential to transform the financial landscape in India. It can bring about greater transparency, enhance security, and streamline processes, contributing to a more efficient and trustworthy financial ecosystem.

Collaborative Efforts for Blockchain Adoption

Successful implementation of blockchain requires a collaborative approach. This involves partnerships between technology providers, financial institutions, regulatory bodies, and other stakeholders. Establishing common standards and protocols is crucial for interoperability and to harness the full potential of blockchain across different sectors.

Educational Initiatives and Skill Development

To foster the growth of blockchain technology, there is a need for educational initiatives and skill development programs. This will equip professionals with the necessary knowledge and skills to develop and manage blockchain applications effectively.

The blockchain revolution in India is not just about cryptocurrency; it's about leveraging a groundbreaking technology to redefine the financial sector's landscape. From banking and insurance to government transactions and beyond, blockchain holds the promise of a more transparent, secure, and efficient financial system. As India continues to explore and embrace this technology, it stands on the cusp of a major financial transformation that goes far beyond the boundaries of traditional finance.

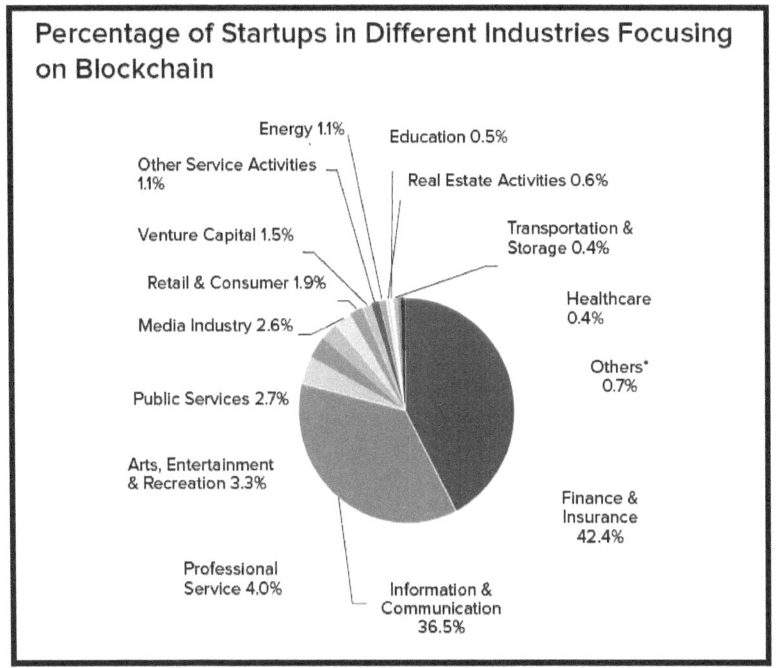

Blockchain Revolution

"India's journey in FinTech: Where tradition meets innovation, and challenges pave the way for opportunities."

୫୬

V

Peer-to-Peer Lending: Democratizing Credit

Understanding the Rise and Mechanism of P2P Lending Platforms

Peer-to-Peer (P2P) lending has emerged as a pivotal component in the FinTech landscape of India, revolutionizing the traditional credit system. This chapter delves into how P2P lending platforms have democratized access to credit, offering an alternative to the conventional banking and financial institutions.

The Emergence of P2P Lending

P2P lending, at its core, is a system where individuals can directly lend to other individuals or businesses without the need for a traditional financial intermediary like a bank. This concept gained traction in India with the advent of FinTech, spurred by the growing internet penetration and the desire for more accessible lending and borrowing methods.

How P2P Lending Works

P2P platforms function as online marketplaces, connecting borrowers with potential lenders. Borrowers list their loan requirements, and lenders, attracted by the prospect of higher returns compared to traditional savings, can fund these loans either partially or fully. The P2P platform facilitates this exchange, ensuring both parties' security and compliance with regulatory standards.

Advantages Over Traditional Lending

P2P lending offers several advantages over traditional credit systems. For borrowers, it provides easier access to funds, often with less stringent eligibility criteria than banks. For lenders, it offers an opportunity to earn higher returns on their investments. The entire process is typically faster, more transparent, and user-friendly than conventional banking channels.

Credit Inclusion

One of the most significant impacts of P2P lending is financial inclusion. It has opened doors for segments of the population who were previously underserved or excluded by traditional financial institutions, such as small entrepreneurs, individuals with no formal credit history, and those in rural areas.

Risk Management and Due Diligence

While P2P lending offers many advantages, it also carries risks, primarily credit risk. To mitigate this, P2P platforms employ sophisticated risk assessment tools, leveraging data analytics and

AI to evaluate borrowers' creditworthiness. They also provide diversification options for lenders, spreading the risk across multiple loans.

Regulatory Framework

The Reserve Bank of India (RBI) has set regulations for P2P lending to ensure a stable and secure ecosystem. These regulations include caps on individual lender exposure, requirements for fair practices, and measures for data security and grievance redressal.

Challenges and Future Prospects

Despite its growth, P2P lending faces challenges such as building trust among users, managing default rates, and adapting to evolving regulatory frameworks. However, the future looks promising,

with the potential for technological advancements to further enhance the efficiency and reach of P2P platforms. Integration with India's digital identification system (Aadhaar) and the Unified Payments Interface (UPI) could streamline processes further, making P2P lending even more accessible.

The potential of P2P lending to transform the credit landscape in India is immense. As technology continues to evolve and regulatory frameworks become more robust, P2P platforms are likely to become a significant part of India's financial ecosystem. They not only offer an alternative to traditional banking but also empower individuals to be both consumers and providers of financial services, thus democratizing credit in the truest sense.

The Road Ahead

Looking forward, P2P lending is poised to play a crucial role in shaping India's financial inclusion story. With its ability to reach the unbanked and underbanked segments, it complements the government's efforts to ensure access to financial services for all. The model also presents an opportunity for innovative financial products tailored to the diverse needs of India's population.

In summary, P2P lending in India represents a paradigm shift in the way credit is perceived and accessed. It's not just about providing an alternative lending platform; it's about creating a more inclusive financial system where credit is accessible, transparent, and efficient.

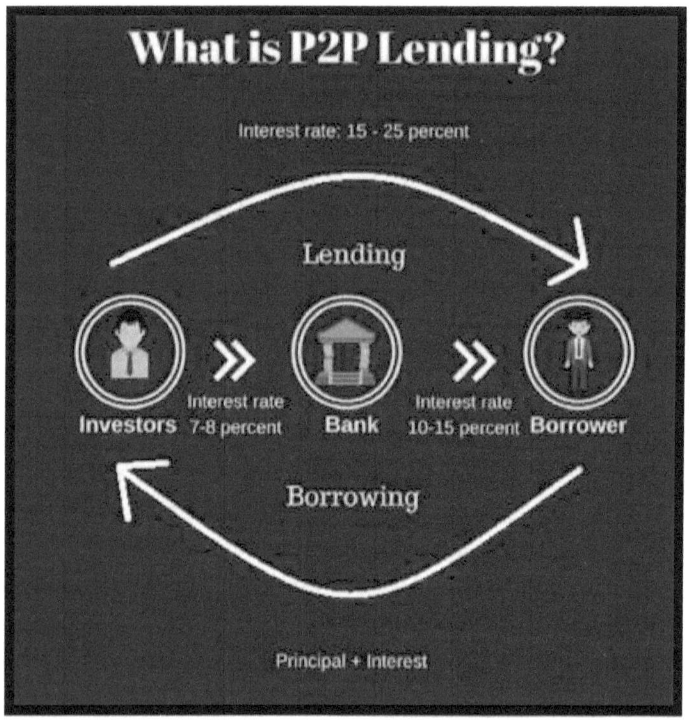

P2P Lending

● 31 ●

"In the heart of India's FinTech revolution lies a simple promise: Finance for all."

ॐ

VI

Crowdfunding: A New Era of Investment

Examining How Crowdfunding is Reshaping Investment in Startups

Crowdfunding has emerged as a revolutionary force in the investment world, especially for startups in India. This chapter explores how this innovative approach to raising capital is reshaping the landscape of startup financing, offering an alternative to traditional funding methods.

The Concept of Crowdfunding

Crowdfunding is a method of raising capital through the collective effort of a large number of individuals, typically via the internet. This approach democratizes the investment process, allowing anyone to contribute small amounts of capital to support a business, project, or social cause.

Types of Crowdfunding

There are several types of crowdfunding, each serving a different purpose:

Reward-Based Crowdfunding: Backers receive a tangible item or service in return for their funds.

Equity Crowdfunding: Investors receive a stake in the company.

Debt Crowdfunding: Also known as peer-to-peer lending, where backers lend money with the expectation of repayment with interest.

Donation-Based Crowdfunding: Funds are raised for charitable causes without any expectation of return.

Crowdfunding in India: The Startup Booster

For Indian startups, crowdfunding has become an attractive option. It not only provides access to capital but also serves as a platform for market validation and community building. Crowdfunding campaigns allow startups to test their ideas, gather feedback, and generate buzz, all while securing funds.

Success Stories and Impact

Several Indian startups have successfully leveraged crowdfunding platforms to kickstart their ventures. These success stories have not only brought innovative products and services to the market but have also inspired a new generation of entrepreneurs to follow suit.

Regulatory Landscape

The Securities and Exchange Board of India (SEBI) has been monitoring the crowdfunding landscape to ensure investor protection while fostering a conducive environment for this form of fundraising. The evolving regulatory framework is aimed at balancing the need for innovation with the necessity of financial oversight.

Challenges and Opportunities

Despite its potential, crowdfunding in India faces challenges. These include limited public awareness, varying levels of internet access, and concerns about project viability and platform credibility. However, these challenges also present opportunities for growth and development in the sector, such as the potential for technological innovation and the creation of more robust due diligence processes.

Crowdfunding and Financial Inclusion

Crowdfunding also plays a significant role in financial inclusion, allowing individuals from varied socio-economic backgrounds to participate in investment opportunities that were once reserved for a select few. This inclusivity has the potential to create a more diverse and resilient economic landscape.

The Future of Crowdfunding in India

Looking ahead, crowdfunding is set to become an increasingly significant player in India's investment ecosystem, particularly for startups. As technology advances and regulatory frameworks evolve, crowdfunding is expected to become more accessible, efficient, and secure.

Crowdfunding represents a paradigm shift in how startups are funded and how individuals can participate in the investment process. It embodies the spirit of collective support and financial democracy, enabling a wide array of ideas and ventures to come to fruition. This chapter not only sheds light on the current state of crowdfunding in India but also offers a glimpse into its promising future as a transformative tool for investment and innovation.

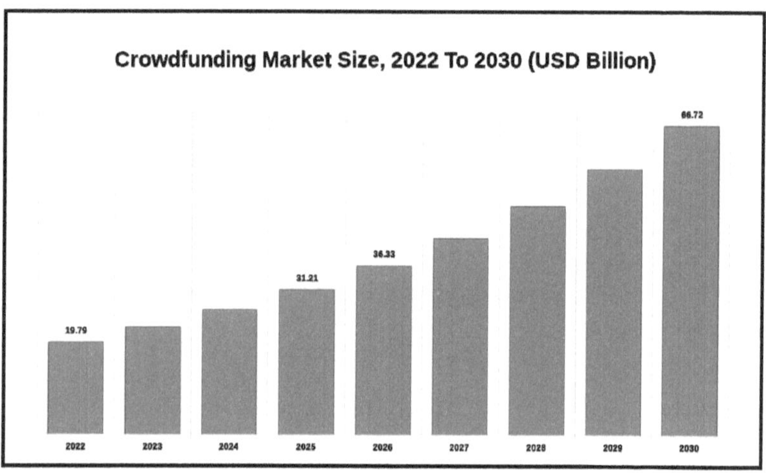

Crowdfundng Market

"Embracing FinTech in India means embracing change for a better, more inclusive economy."

క్ర

VII

Financial Inclusion: Bridging the Gap with Technology

The Role of FinTech in Enhancing Financial Inclusion in India

Financial inclusion, the process of ensuring access to essential financial services for all segments of society, particularly the underprivileged and underbanked, is a critical goal in India.

Understanding Financial Inclusion in the Indian Context

India, with its diverse and vast population, presents unique challenges in achieving financial inclusion. A significant portion of the population has historically been excluded from the formal financial system due to reasons like lack of documentation, financial literacy, and access to banking facilities.

The Digital Leap

The advent of FinTech in India has catalyzed a digital leap in financial services. With the proliferation of smartphones and the internet, FinTech solutions have become more accessible. Digital platforms now offer a range of services like basic banking, digital payments, insurance, and lending, even in remote areas.

Mobile Wallets and Payments

Mobile wallets and payment apps have been instrumental in driving financial inclusion. They allow users to perform transactions, pay bills, and transfer money without needing a traditional bank account. This convenience has brought countless new users into the fold of digital finance.

Microfinance and Microloans

FinTech platforms have revolutionized microfinance, offering small loans to those traditionally deemed un-bankable. By using alternative data and AI for credit scoring, these platforms can assess the creditworthiness of individuals without traditional credit histories, thereby extending credit to new segments.

Government Initiatives and Collaboration

The Indian government has been a key player in promoting financial inclusion through technology. Initiatives like the Jan Dhan Yojana, Aadhaar, and the Unified Payments Interface (UPI) have laid the foundation for a more inclusive financial ecosystem. Collaborations between the government and FinTech companies are further enhancing the reach and efficiency of financial services.

Overcoming Challenges

Despite the progress, challenges remain. Issues like digital literacy, cybersecurity, and internet connectivity continue to hinder the full potential of FinTech in achieving financial inclusion. Addressing these challenges requires concerted efforts from the government, FinTech sector, and other stakeholders.

The Role of Education and Awareness

Educational initiatives focusing on digital literacy and financial education are crucial in making financial inclusion efforts more effective. Understanding how to use FinTech services safely and wisely is as important as accessing them.

Looking Forward

The future of financial inclusion in India through FinTech is promising but requires continuous innovation and adaptation. The integration of advanced technologies like blockchain and AI could further enhance the security and efficiency of financial services, making them more accessible to the underserved segments of the population.

The Social Impact of Financial Inclusion

The social impact of FinTech-led financial inclusion cannot be overstated. By providing access to financial services, FinTech is empowering individuals and small businesses, fostering entrepreneurship, and contributing to overall economic growth. This inclusion also plays a critical role in reducing poverty and promoting social equality.

Building a Resilient Financial Ecosystem

The journey towards a fully inclusive financial system is about building resilience and stability. FinTech, with its innovative solutions, has the potential to create a financial ecosystem that is not only inclusive but also resilient to economic fluctuations and crises.

FinTech's role in enhancing financial inclusion in India is a testament to the power of technology in transforming lives. As we move forward, the focus should remain on innovating and adapting these technologies to meet the diverse needs of India's population. This chapter not only highlights the achievements and potential of FinTech in bridging the financial gap but also underscores the ongoing efforts and future strategies needed to realize the vision of a financially inclusive India.

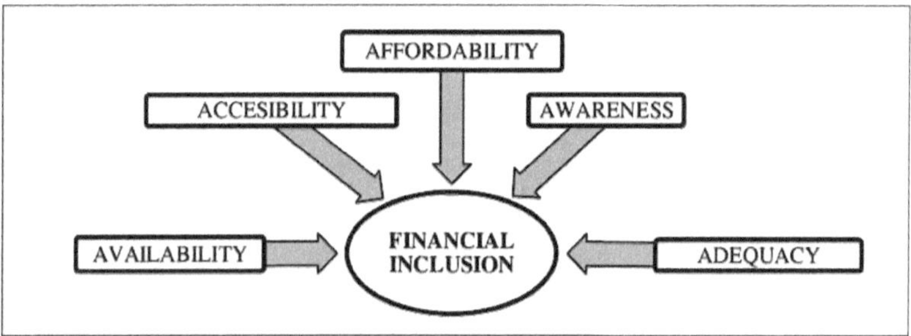

Financial Inclusion

"FinTech in India: A dance of technology and tradition, leading the march towards financial empowerment."

ॐ

VIII

Regulatory Landscapes: Navigating Compliance and Innovation

Discussion on Regulations, Compliance, and the Challenges They Pose

In the rapidly evolving world of FinTech in India, regulatory frameworks play a crucial role in shaping the ecosystem's growth. This chapter delves into the intricacies of navigating compliance and innovation within the regulatory landscapes that govern FinTech.

The Importance of Regulation in FinTech

Regulation in FinTech is essential for ensuring financial stability, consumer protection, and the prevention of fraud and money laundering. However, the fast-paced nature of technological innovation in FinTech often outpaces the development of regulatory frameworks, leading to a complex interplay between compliance and innovation.

The Indian Regulatory Framework

The Reserve Bank of India (RBI) and the Securities and Exchange Board of India (SEBI) are the primary regulators overseeing FinTech in India. Their guidelines and directives aim to create a balanced environment that fosters innovation while ensuring financial system integrity and customer protection.

Key Regulatory Initiatives

The Payment and Settlement Systems Act, 2007: This act provides a framework for payment systems in India and has been instrumental in regulating digital payment services.

Guidelines on Digital Lending: Aimed at addressing the challenges posed by the digital lending ecosystem, these guidelines focus on ensuring fair practices and protecting borrowers.

Regulatory Sandbox: RBI's introduction of a regulatory sandbox allows FinTech companies to test their innovations in a controlled environment, balancing the need for innovation with regulatory compliance.

Challenges in Compliance

One of the major challenges faced by FinTech firms is staying compliant with existing regulations, which

can sometimes be complex and constantly evolving. This can be particularly daunting for startups with limited resources. Moreover, navigating the nuances of regulations that were primarily designed for traditional financial institutions can be tricky for these technology-driven entities.

Balancing Innovation and Regulation

There is a delicate balance to be struck between fostering innovation and ensuring robust regulation. Too much regulation can stifle innovation and hinder growth, while too little can lead to risks in financial stability and consumer protection. Policymakers face the challenge of updating and adapting regulations to keep pace with technological advancements.

The Role of Self-Regulation

In addition to government-imposed regulations, there's an increasing focus on self-regulation within the FinTech industry. Industry-led standards and best practices can play a significant role in ensuring responsible growth and building trust among consumers.

Global Perspectives and Learning

India's regulatory approach to FinTech can benefit from global perspectives. Learning from the regulatory frameworks of other countries, which have faced similar challenges, can provide valuable insights for shaping effective policies.

The Future of FinTech Regulation

Looking forward, the regulatory landscape for FinTech in India is expected to evolve continuously. It will need to accommodate emerging technologies like blockchain and artificial intelligence while addressing new challenges such as data privacy and cybersecurity.

Collaboration is Key

Effective regulation of FinTech requires collaboration between regulators, FinTech companies, traditional financial institutions, and other stakeholders. Open dialogue and partnership can lead to more informed and effective policy-making.

Navigating the regulatory landscape is a critical aspect of the FinTech ecosystem in India. While it poses challenges, effective regulation is fundamental to the health and growth of the FinTech sector. This chapter not only examines the current state of FinTech regulation but also provides a forward-looking perspective on how regulation can evolve to continue supporting innovation while ensuring a safe and stable financial environment.

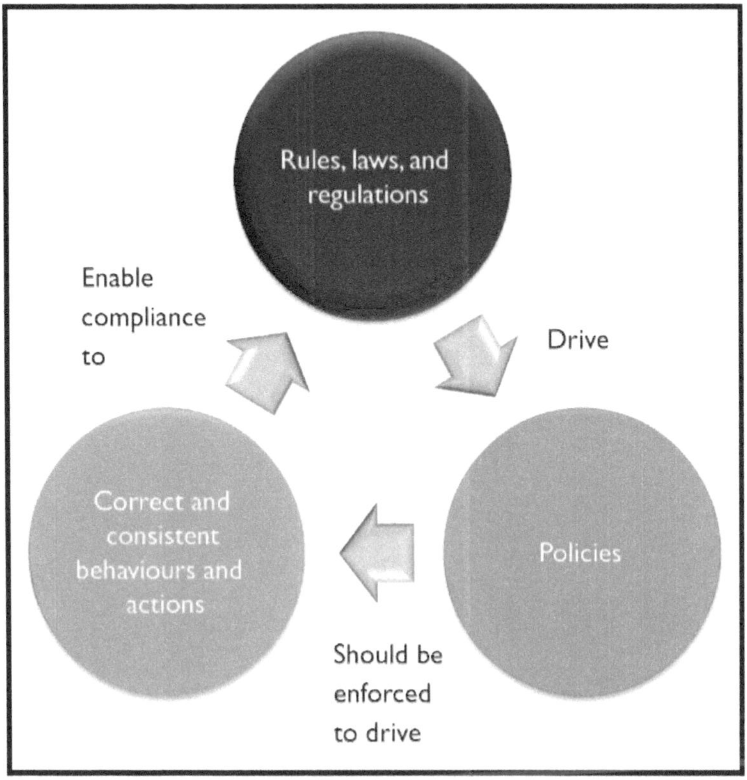

Data Governance and Compliance

"Every digital wallet in India's FinTech landscape is a testament to the country's unyielding spirit of progress."

৪৩

IX

Cybersecurity in FinTech: Safeguarding the Digital Frontier

Focus on the Importance of Cybersecurity Measures in FinTech

As the FinTech sector in India grows and evolves, cybersecurity emerges as a critical concern. This chapter delves into the importance of robust cybersecurity measures in safeguarding the financial data and transactions that form the backbone of the FinTech industry.

The Cybersecurity Imperative in FinTech

FinTech, by its very nature, involves the handling of sensitive financial data and large-scale monetary transactions. This makes it a prime target for cyber threats like data breaches, hacking, phishing, and other forms of cyberattacks. The trust and credibility of FinTech services hinge significantly on their ability to protect against these threats.

Understanding the Threat Landscape

The threat landscape in the digital finance sector is constantly evolving, with cybercriminals employing increasingly sophisticated methods. This includes everything from advanced malware and ransomware attacks to social engineering tactics. Staying ahead of these threats requires a deep understanding of the cybersecurity domain.

Regulatory Compliance and Standards

In India, regulatory bodies like the Reserve Bank of India (RBI) and the Securities and Exchange Board of India (SEBI) have laid down guidelines and standards for cybersecurity in the financial sector. Compliance with these regulations is not just a legal requirement but also a crucial aspect of building user trust.

Building a Robust Cybersecurity Framework

A robust cybersecurity framework in FinTech involves multiple layers of defense. This includes secure infrastructure, encryption, access controls, regular security audits, and real-time monitoring systems. In addition, employing advanced technologies like artificial intelligence and machine learning can enhance threat detection and response.

The Human Element

While technology is at the forefront of cybersecurity, the human element cannot be overlooked. Employee training and awareness programs are essential in minimizing risks posed by human error and insider threats. Building a culture of security within organizations is as important as deploying technological solutions.

Data Privacy and Protection

With the increasing concern about data privacy, FinTech companies must ensure the confidentiality and integrity of customer data. Adherence to data protection laws, such as the Personal Data Protection Bill in India, is crucial for maintaining customer trust and regulatory compliance.

Cyber Resilience

Cyber resilience involves not only protecting against cyber threats but also having the capability to quickly recover and resume operations in the event of a breach. This includes having robust incident response plans and disaster recovery strategies.

Collaboration and Information Sharing

Collaboration between FinTech companies, cybersecurity experts, and

regulatory authorities is key in building a strong defense against cyber threats. Sharing information about potential threats, vulnerabilities, and best practices can help in creating a more secure FinTech ecosystem.

Investing in Cybersecurity

Investment in cybersecurity is not just a cost; it's a critical investment in the company's future. FinTech firms must allocate adequate resources for cybersecurity measures to protect their business and their customers.

The Role of Emerging Technologies

Emerging technologies like blockchain and biometric authentication are playing an increasingly significant role in enhancing cybersecurity in FinTech. These technologies offer new ways to secure transactions and protect data.

Challenges and Opportunities

While cybersecurity poses significant challenges to the FinTech sector, it also presents opportunities for innovation. Developing new security solutions and technologies can give a competitive edge to FinTech firms and contribute to the overall growth of the sector.

In the rapidly evolving world of FinTech, cybersecurity is not just a technical issue but a fundamental business imperative. It forms the core of customer trust and the resilience of the financial system. This chapter emphasizes the importance of cybersecurity in FinTech, outlining the threats, strategies, and best practices that are essential in safeguarding the digital frontier of finance. As the FinTech landscape continues to expand and diversify, the role of cybersecurity will become increasingly central to its sustainability and success.

Benefits of Cybersecurity in Fintech

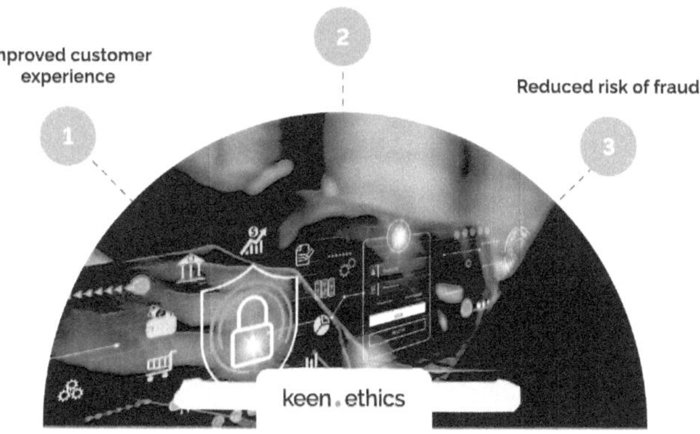

"India's FinTech story is written in code, but it
reads like a tale of dreams and determination."

‽

X

Artificial Intelligence in Finance: The Smart Money

How AI and Machine Learning are Transforming Financial Services

Artificial Intelligence (AI) and Machine Learning (ML) are at the forefront of the technological revolution in the financial sector. This chapter explores the transformative impact of these technologies on financial services, detailing how they are reshaping the industry in India.

The Advent of AI in Finance

The integration of AI in finance has been driven by the need for more efficient, accurate, and customer-centric services. From risk assessment and fraud detection to personalized financial advice, AI is enabling financial institutions to operate smarter and more effectively.

AI in Risk Management and Fraud Detection

One of the most significant applications of AI in finance is in the realm of risk management and fraud detection. By analyzing vast amounts of data and recognizing patterns that may indicate fraudulent activities, AI systems can identify potential risks and threats much faster and more accurately than traditional methods.

Machine Learning in Credit Scoring

Machine Learning algorithms have revolutionized the way credit scores are determined. By analyzing non-traditional data sources such as online transactions, social media activities, and mobile app usage, these algorithms can provide a more comprehensive and nuanced assessment of a borrower's creditworthiness, especially beneficial for individuals with limited credit history.

Algorithmic Trading

AI and ML have also transformed trading in financial markets. Algorithmic trading uses complex AI models to make fast, efficient, and informed trading decisions. This has led to more liquid and efficient markets, though it also raises concerns about market stability and the ethical implications of automated trading.

Personalized Banking and Robo-Advisors

AI is making banking more personal and accessible. AI-powered chatbots provide customer support and financial advice, while robo-advisors offer

automated, algorithm-driven financial planning services with minimal human supervision. These technologies are democratizing financial advice, making it accessible to a broader audience at a lower cost.

Enhancing Customer Experience

AI-driven tools are being used to enhance the customer experience in banking and finance. From personalized product recommendations to predictive analytics for customizing financial solutions, AI enables a more tailored approach to customer service.

Operational Efficiency

AI and ML are streamlining operational processes in financial institutions. Tasks like document verification, compliance checks, and report generation, which traditionally required significant manpower, can now be automated for greater efficiency and accuracy.

The Role of Data

The power of AI in finance is largely dependent on data. The quality, quantity, and diversity of data play a crucial role in the effectiveness of AI and ML models. This reliance on data raises important questions about privacy, data security, and ethical data usage.

Overcoming Challenges

Despite its advantages, the integration of AI in finance faces challenges. These include data privacy concerns, the need for regulatory frameworks tailored to AI technologies, and the potential for biases in AI algorithms. Addressing these challenges requires a collaborative approach involving industry stakeholders, regulatory bodies, and technology experts.

The Future of AI in Finance

Looking ahead, AI and ML are poised to drive further innovation in financial services. Emerging trends such as deep learning, neural networks, and natural language processing (NLP) will likely unveil new possibilities in financial analysis, customer interaction, and risk management.

AI and ML are not just reshaping the financial services industry; they are redefining its future. "The Smart Money" in finance is increasingly data-driven, automated, and intelligent. This chapter underscores the transformative impact of AI and ML in finance, highlighting both the opportunities and challenges they present. As the FinTech landscape continues to evolve, AI and ML will remain central to its growth, driving innovation and efficiency in an increasingly digital financial world.

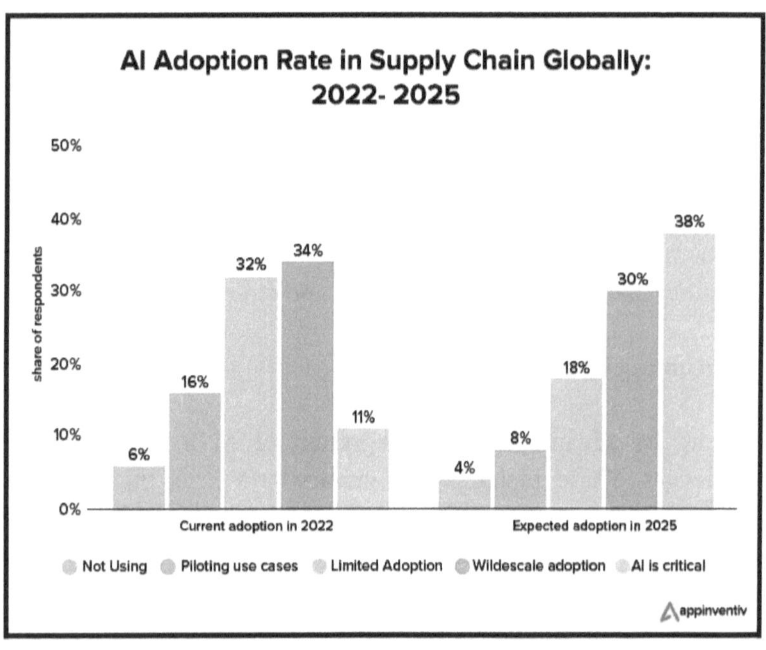

AI Adoption Rate in Supply Chain Globally

"In the face of adversity, India's FinTech finds not
just solutions, but also opportunities."

࿐

XI

Mobile Wallets: The Convenience Factor

Growth and Impact of Mobile Wallet Services

In the digital age, mobile wallets have become synonymous with convenience in financial transactions. This chapter explores the meteoric rise of mobile wallet services in India, examining their profound impact on the way financial transactions are conducted.

The Surge of Mobile Wallets in India

The journey of mobile wallets in India is a story of remarkable growth, largely fueled by the increasing penetration of smartphones and the internet. The convenience of conducting transactions with just a few taps has made mobile wallets immensely popular among India's tech-savvy population.

The Role of Demonetization

The demonetization initiative in 2016 acted as a catalyst in the adoption of mobile wallets. With a sudden reduction in cash availability, consumers and merchants alike turned to mobile wallets as a convenient alternative, significantly boosting their usage and acceptance.

Diverse Applications

Mobile wallets in India have transcended beyond mere payment instruments. They are now used for a wide range of transactions, including bill payments, money transfers, online shopping, and even for financial services like loans and insurance. The integration of mobile wallets with UPI (Unified Payments Interface) has further expanded their functionality and ease of use.

Impact on Retail and E-commerce

The proliferation of mobile wallets has transformed the retail and e-commerce landscape in India. They have enabled seamless and swift transactions, contributing to the growth of online shopping and benefiting both consumers and businesses with improved efficiency and reduced transaction costs.

Financial Inclusion

Mobile wallets have played a significant role in advancing financial inclusion in India. They have provided an entry point into the formal financial system for the unbanked and underbanked populations, especially in rural and semi-urban areas where traditional banking infrastructure is limited.

User Experience and Innovation

The success of mobile wallets hinges on the user experience they offer. Continual innovation in terms of user interface, security features, and value-added services is key to retaining and expanding their user base. Features like cashback offers, rewards, and loyalty programs have also contributed to their popularity.

Security Concerns

As with any digital financial service, security is a paramount concern with mobile wallets. Ensuring robust security protocols and educating users about safe usage practices are essential to maintain trust and prevent fraud.

Regulatory Environment

The regulatory environment in India has been evolving

to keep pace with the growth of mobile wallets. The Reserve Bank of India (RBI) has introduced guidelines to ensure the safety and security of transactions, mandating KYC (Know Your Customer) norms, and setting transaction limits to mitigate risks.

Partnership and Integration

Mobile wallets have seen a trend of partnerships and integrations, both with traditional financial institutions and other businesses. These collaborations have expanded the reach and utility of mobile wallets, allowing for a more integrated financial ecosystem.

The Future of Mobile Wallets

Looking forward, mobile wallets are expected to continue evolving, integrating more advanced technologies like biometric authentication and artificial intelligence to enhance user experience and security. They are poised to play a significant role in the future of digital payments and financial services in India.

Mobile wallets have not just added convenience to financial

transactions; they have revolutionized them. They embody the shift towards a more digital, efficient, and inclusive financial landscape in India. As mobile wallet usage continues to soar, they will undoubtedly remain a cornerstone of India's FinTech revolution.

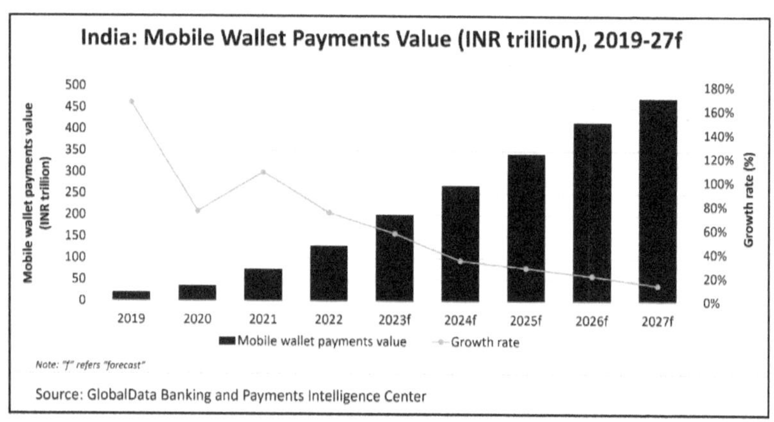

Mobile Wallet Payments - India

"India's FinTech is not just growing; it's thriving,
driven by innovation and inclusive aspirations."

৪৩

XII

InsurTech: Redefining Insurance in India

Exploring the Intersection of Technology and Insurance

InsurTech, a blend of 'insurance' and 'technology', is radically transforming the insurance sector in India. This chapter delves into how technological innovations are redefining insurance, making it more accessible, efficient, and tailored to the modern consumer.

The Emergence of InsurTech

The InsurTech revolution in India is part of a global trend that sees technology infiltrating traditional insurance models. Driven by advancements in digital technology, InsurTech in India is reshaping how insurance products are designed, priced, sold, and serviced.

Customized Insurance Products

One of the hallmarks of InsurTech is the ability to offer customized insurance products. Leveraging big data and analytics, insurers can now create personalized insurance policies based on individual risk profiles, changing the one-size-fits-all approach to a more tailored experience.

Streamlining Processes

Technology has streamlined many insurance processes, making them more efficient and user-friendly. From online policy comparison and purchase to digital claim filing and processing, InsurTech is eliminating many of the traditional pain points in the insurance journey.

The Role of AI and Machine Learning

Artificial Intelligence (AI) and Machine Learning (ML) are at the forefront of the InsurTech revolution. They enable advanced risk assessment, fraud detection, and automated customer service through chatbots. These technologies are not only improving operational efficiency but also enhancing customer engagement.

Blockchain in Insurance

Blockchain technology is beginning to find applications in the insurance sector. With its features of transparency, security, and immutability, blockchain can potentially revolutionize areas like policy issuance, claims processing, and fraud prevention in insurance.

The Growth of Telematics

In sectors like auto insurance, telematics is becoming increasingly popular. By using devices to track vehicle usage and driving behavior, insurers can offer usage-based insurance (UBI), which is more fair and accurate than traditional methods.

Impact on Health Insurance

In health insurance, wearable technology and health apps are enabling insurers to monitor policyholders' health metrics in real time. This data can be used to offer incentives for healthy behavior, tailor health insurance packages, and streamline the claims process.

Regulatory Challenges

The InsurTech industry faces regulatory challenges as it navig

ates a sector traditionally governed by strict regulations. Ensuring compliance while fostering innovation is a delicate balance. The regulatory bodies in India are evolving their frameworks to accommodate these new technological advancements while protecting consumer interests.

Cybersecurity and Data Privacy

As insurance companies collect and store vast amounts of personal data, cybersecurity and data privacy become paramount. InsurTech companies must ensure robust data protection measures to maintain customer trust and comply with regulations like the Personal Data Protection Bill.

Bridging the Insurance Gap

InsurTech has the potential to bridge the significant insurance gap in India by making insurance products more accessible and affordable. With digital platforms and mobile applications, insurance can reach a wider audience, including those in rural and remote areas.

The Future of InsurTech

The future of InsurTech in India is marked by immense potential. Emerging technologies like the Internet of Things (IoT), advanced analytics, and the further integration of AI and ML are expected to continue driving innovation in this space.

InsurTech is redefining the insurance industry in India, making it more aligned with the needs and expectations of the modern consumer. It's not just about technology for technology's sake; it's about leveraging these advancements to create a more inclusive, efficient, and customer-centric insurance ecosystem. This chapter not only explores the current state of InsurTech in India but also provides a glimpse into its promising future, where technology continues to transform the very fabric of the insurance sector.

Steps in insurance fraud detection using big data analysis

Using analytics for insurance fraud detection

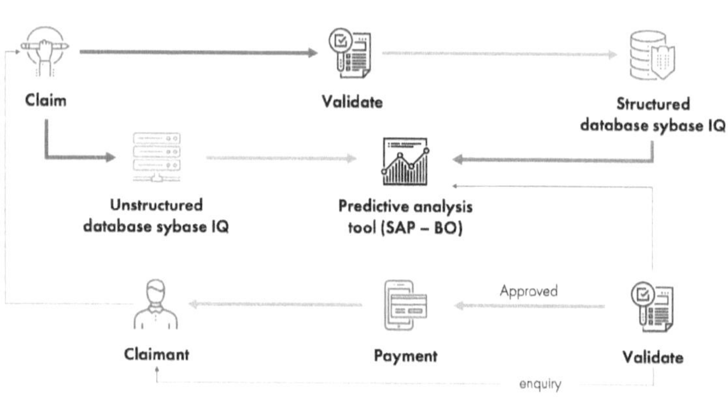

Source: the-digital-insurer.com

"FinTech in India: Fueling dreams with digital dollars and financial inclusion."

೮౩

XIII
WealthTech: Personal Finance Management

Discussing Tools and Platforms for Personal Wealth Management

WealthTech, a contraction of 'wealth' and 'technology', represents the intersection of technology and personal finance management. This chapter explores the various tools and platforms that are reshaping the way individuals manage their wealth in India.

The Rise of WealthTech in India

The WealthTech sector in India has seen significant growth, driven by the increasing demand for personal finance management solutions among the growing middle class and tech-savvy younger generation. With the proliferation of smartphones and internet access, more people are turning to digital solutions for managing their finances.

Robo-Advisors: Democratizing Wealth Management

Robo-advisors are one of the most prominent innovations in

WealthTech. These digital platforms provide automated, algorithm-driven financial planning services with minimal human intervention. They offer personalized investment advice based on the user's financial goals, risk tolerance, and investment horizon, making wealth management accessible to a broader audience.

Budgeting and Savings Apps

There is a wide array of mobile applications designed for budgeting and savings. These apps help users track their spending, set budget goals, and even automatically save small amounts of money. Features like expense categorization, financial insights, and real-time notifications help users stay on top of their finances.

Investment Platforms

Digital investment platforms have revolutionized the way individuals invest in stocks, mutual funds, and other financial instruments. These platforms offer user-friendly interfaces, educational resources, and lower fees compared to traditional investment methods, making investing more accessible to the general public.

Personal Finance Analytics

Advanced analytics tools in WealthTech platforms can analyze users' financial data to provide insights into spending patterns, investment performance, and potential savings opportunities. This data-driven approach helps users make more informed financial decisions.

Integration with Banking Services

Many WealthTech platforms are integrating with traditional banking services, allowing users to have a holistic view of their financial status. This integration includes checking and savings accounts, investments, loans, and credit cards, providing a comprehensive financial management ecosystem.

Security and Privacy Concerns

As with any digital financial service, security and privacy are paramount in WealthTech. Platforms must ensure the highest levels of data encryption and comply with regulations to protect user data from unauthorized access and breaches.

Challenges and Opportunities

WealthTech in India faces challenges such as financial literacy, digital divide, and regulatory compliance. However, these challenges also present opportunities for growth and innovation in the sector.

The Future of WealthTech

The future of WealthTech is promising, with potential advancements in AI, machine learning, and predictive analytics offering even more personalized and sophisticated financial management tools. Integration with emerging technologies like blockchain could further enhance security and transparency in WealthTech services.

WealthTech is transforming personal finance management in India, making it more accessible, efficient, and user-friendly. This chapter highlights the various tools and platforms available for personal wealth management, reflecting the shift towards a more tech-driven approach in managing personal

finances. As technology continues to evolve, WealthTech is poised to play an increasingly significant role in empowering individuals to take control of their financial health, driving a more financially informed and savvy society. This revolution in personal finance management is not just about convenience; it's about harnessing the power of technology to create smarter, more informed financial habits and decisions, contributing to overall economic wellbeing and growth.

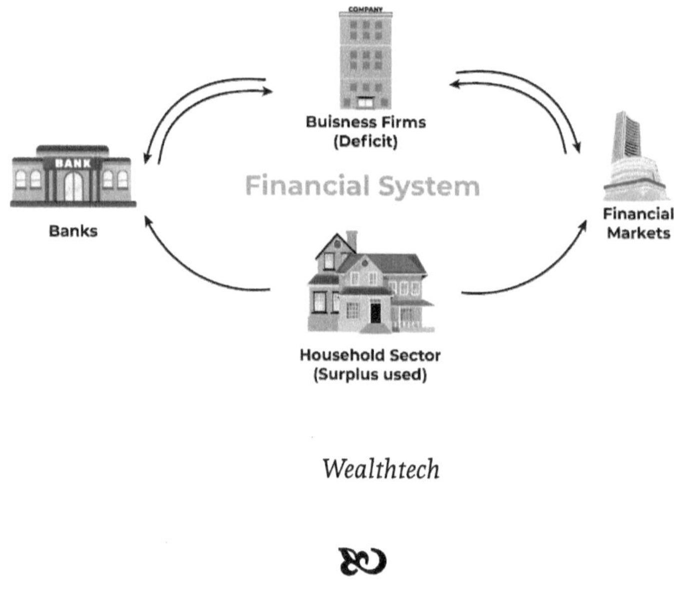

Wealthtech

"India's FinTech revolution is a beacon of hope, illuminating the path to financial literacy and freedom."

౫

XIV

Neobanks: The Future of Banking?"

Analysis of the Rise of Digital-Only Banks in India

Neobanks, or digital-only banks, represent a significant shift in the banking paradigm. This chapter delves into the emergence and growth of neobanks in India, examining their potential to redefine the future of banking in the country.

What are Neobanks?

Neobanks are financial institutions that operate exclusively online without traditional physical branch networks. They offer a range of banking services through digital platforms, including mobile apps. Known for their user-friendly interfaces, neobanks focus on providing efficient, accessible, and cost-effective banking solutions.

The Emergence of Neobanks in India

The rise of neobanks in India is part of a global trend towards digital banking solutions. In India, this movement has been fueled by the rapid digitalization of the economy, increased smartphone penetration, and a young, tech-savvy population seeking convenient and innovative banking services.

Key Features of Neobanks

User Experience: Neobanks offer a seamless and intuitive user experience, with simple account opening procedures, real-time transactions, and personalized customer service.

Technology-Driven: Leveraging cutting-edge technologies like AI, machine learning, and data analytics, neobanks provide tailored financial products and insights to their customers.

Cost-Effectiveness: With lower operational costs compared to traditional banks, neobanks often offer more competitive rates and lower fees.

Impact on Traditional Banking

Neobanks are challenging the traditional banking model by offering more agile and customer-centric services. Their rise is pushing conventional banks to accelerate their digital transformation efforts to stay competitive.

Financial Inclusion

One of the most significant impacts of neobanks is the potential to enhance financial inclusion. By eliminating the need for physical infrastructure, neobanks can reach underserved and unbanked populations, especially in remote areas.

Regulatory Landscape

The regulatory environment for neobanks in India is evolving.

While they are currently required to partner with licensed banks to offer certain services, there is ongoing discussion about introducing a framework specifically for digital-only banking.

Challenges and Risks

Neobanks face challenges such as building customer trust, ensuring data security, and navigating a complex regulatory environment. As entirely digital entities, they also need to be prepared for operational risks like system outages or cyber attacks.

The Future Outlook

The future of neobanks in India looks promising but will depend on various factors, including regulatory developments, technological advancements, and the ability to build sustainable business models. As they continue to grow, neobanks could significantly transform the banking landscape, offering more personalized, efficient, and inclusive banking services.

Neobanks represent a new era in banking, driven by technology and changing consumer preferences. They have the potential to not just complement, but in some areas, lead the banking sector in India. This chapter provides an in-depth analysis of the rise of digital-only banks, exploring their impact, challenges, and the potential to reshape the future of banking in India. As the digital economy grows, neobanks could very well be at the forefront of this transformation, redefining what banking means for millions of customers.

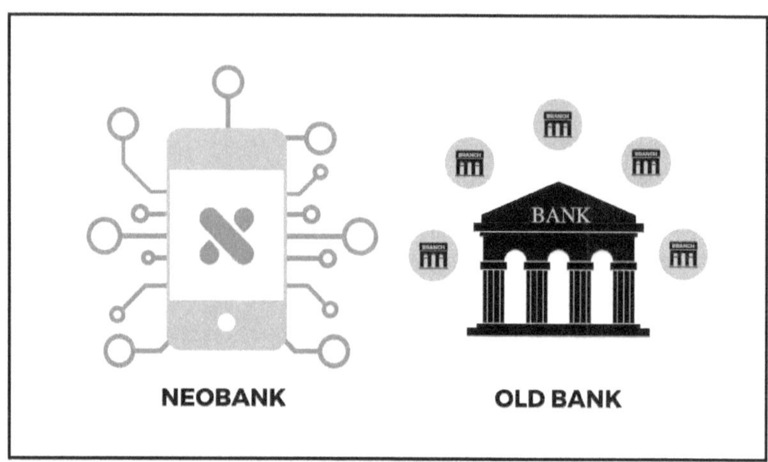

Neobanks

"The pulse of India's economy is increasingly digital, and FinTech is its heartbeat."

☙

XV
UPI and its Transformational Impact

Detailed Look at Unified Payments Interface (UPI) System

Unified Payments Interface (UPI) is a system that has revolutionized the way payments are made in India. This chapter provides a detailed exploration of UPI, examining its development, functionality, and the profound impact it has had on the financial landscape of the country.

Background and Development of UPI

UPI was developed by the National Payments Corporation of India (NPCI) as a part of the Indian government's push towards a more digital economy. Launched in 2016, UPI aimed to simplify and unify the myriad of existing payment systems and provide a single, seamless platform for all digital transactions.

How UPI Works

UPI allows users to instantly transfer money between bank accounts using a mobile platform. It operates on a unique identifier, such as a mobile number or virtual payment address, eliminating the need to enter lengthy account details. UPI combines multiple banking features, including seamless fund routing and merchant payments, into one platform.

Key Features of UPI

Interoperability: UPI enables transactions between different banks through its unified interface.

Simplicity: The easy-to-use interface requires minimal data entry from the user.

Real-time Transactions: UPI processes payments in real time, providing instant transfer of funds.

24/7 Availability: It operates round the clock, allowing transactions at any time.

Impact on Digital Payments

UPI has significantly accelerated the adoption of digital payments in India. Its ease of use and efficiency have made it a popular choice for a wide range of transactions, from peer-to-peer transfers to merchant payments. UPI has effectively democratized digital payments, making them accessible to a broader segment of the population.

UPI and Financial Inclusion

UPI has played a crucial role in advancing financial inclusion in

India. By enabling easy and affordable digital transactions, it has brought many first-time users into the digital financial system, especially in rural and semi-urban areas.

The Role in E-Commerce and Retail

UPI has transformed the e-commerce and retail landscape by providing a quick and secure payment method. This has not only enhanced customer convenience but also increased the reliability of cashless transactions for merchants.

Challenges and Future Developments

Despite its success, UPI faces challenges such as managing the increasing volume of transactions and ensuring robust security measures. Future developments in UPI, including the integration of more advanced technologies and expanding international presence, are expected to further enhance its capabilities.

The Unified Payments Interface (UPI) system stands as a testament to India's innovative approach to digital payments. It has not just simplified transactions but has also been a key driver in the country's shift towards a digital economy. This chapter highlights UPI's transformative impact, painting a picture of a future where financial transactions are increasingly seamless, inclusive, and integrated into the everyday lives of millions.

Instant, real time interbank transfer system.
Facilitates inter-bank peer-to-peer (P2P) and person-to-merchant (P2M) transactions.
UPI
UNIFIED PAYMENTS INTERFACE
Open API architecture enabling fintech providers to build application on top of UPI platform.
UPI is mandated a zero-charge framework, ie. No charges levied for users and merchants.

UPI

৩

"In the vibrant landscape of Indian FinTech, every transaction is a step towards a more empowered society."

୫୦

XVI

Challenges in Adoption: The Roadblocks to FinTech Success

Identifying and Addressing Challenges in FinTech Adoption

While the FinTech revolution in India has seen remarkable growth, its path has not been without challenges. This chapter examines the various roadblocks in the adoption of FinTech and explores strategies to address these obstacles.

Regulatory Hurdles

One of the primary challenges facing FinTech in India is navigating the complex regulatory landscape. Regulations that govern financial services were often established in the pre-digital era and may not always align with the innovative nature of FinTech solutions. Balancing compliance while fostering innovation is a key challenge for FinTech companies.

Technological Barriers

Despite India's growing digital footprint, technological barriers such as limited internet connectivity in rural areas and the digital divide pose significant challenges. Ensuring that FinTech services are accessible to all segments of the population, including those with limited tech-savviness, is crucial for widespread adoption.

Cybersecurity Concerns

As FinTech companies handle sensitive financial data, cybersecurity is a major concern. Building robust security systems to protect against data breaches and cyberattacks is imperative. Consumer concerns about the safety of their financial data can also hinder the adoption of FinTech services.

Financial Literacy and Consumer Trust

A significant portion of the Indian population lacks financial literacy, which can be a barrier to understanding and trusting FinTech services. Educating consumers about the benefits and safe usage of FinTech is essential to increase adoption.

Interoperability Challenges

Interoperability between different FinTech services and traditional banking systems is crucial for a seamless customer experience. However, achieving this can be challenging due to differing standards, technologies, and protocols.

Scalability and Sustainability

For FinTech startups, scaling their business while maintaining service quality can be challenging. Furthermore, developing a sustainable business model that balances profitability with the cost of innovative technologies is crucial for long-term success.

User Experience and Design

FinTech companies must focus on user-centric design and experience. A platform's ease of use, interface design, and customer support can significantly impact its adoption rates.

Competition from Traditional Banks

FinTech companies often face stiff competition from traditional banks, which are increasingly adopting digital technologies. Standing out in a crowded market requires continuous innovation and unique value propositions.

Strategies for Overcoming Challenges

To overcome these challenges, FinTech companies need to:

Collaborate closely with regulatory bodies for compliant and innovative solutions.

Invest in cybersecurity and data protection measures.

Engage in consumer education and awareness campaigns.

Focus on building user-friendly and accessible platforms.

Develop scalable and sustainable business models.

The road to FinTech success in India is paved with various challenges, from regulatory hurdles to technological and security concerns. Addressing these issues requires a collaborative approach involving FinTech companies, regulators, traditional financial institutions, and other stakeholders. By overcoming these challenges, FinTech has the potential to further revolutionize the financial sector in India, making it more inclusive, efficient, and customer-centric.

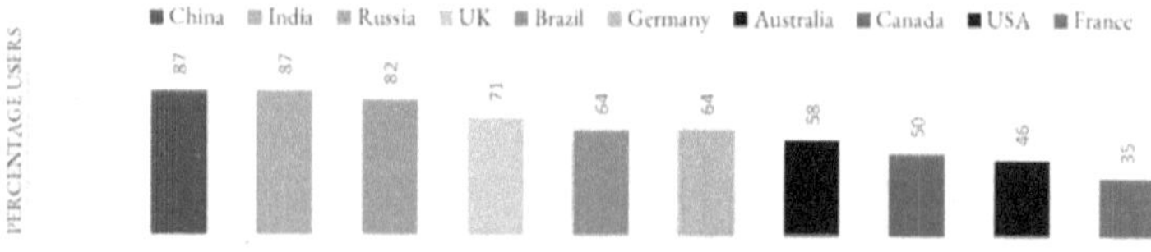

CONSUMER FINTECH ADOPTION ACROSS LEADING MARKETS

Fintech Adoption

*"FinTech in India is rewriting the rules of finance,
one digital innovation at a time."*

☙

XVII

Financial Literacy and Consumer Education

The Importance of Educating Consumers About FinTech Services

In the rapidly evolving FinTech landscape, consumer education and
financial literacy emerge as crucial elements for empowering users
and maximizing the benefits of FinTech services. This chapter
delves into why and how educating consumers about FinTech is
vital for both individuals and the broader financial ecosystem.

Understanding Financial Literacy in the Context of FinTech

Financial literacy in the era of FinTech extends beyond traditional
concepts of saving and investing. It encompasses understanding
digital financial tools, recognizing the risks and benefits of these
services, and making informed decisions about using them.

The Digital Divide and Financial Education

A significant challenge in FinTech adoption is the digital divide.
Many consumers, particularly in rural areas or among older

populations, may not be familiar with digital technology. Educating these groups about using digital financial services safely and effectively is critical for inclusive growth.

The Risks of Low Financial Literacy

Low levels of financial literacy can lead to misuse of FinTech services, susceptibility to fraud, and poor financial decisions. This not only affects individual users but can also have broader implications for the stability and integrity of the financial system.

Strategies for Effective Consumer Education

Collaborative Efforts: Partnerships between FinTech companies, governments, educational institutions, and non-profits can create comprehensive financial literacy programs.

Tailored Content: Financial education content should be tailored to different segments of the population, considering factors like age, socio-economic background, and digital literacy levels.

Leveraging Technology: Utilizing digital platforms and tools for educational purposes can make learning about FinTech services more accessible and engaging.

Incorporating Behavioral Insights: Understanding consumer behavior can help in designing education programs that effectively change financial habits and decision-making.

The Role of Regulators and Policy Makers

Regulators and policymakers play a critical role in promoting financial literacy. They can mandate financial education initiatives as part of FinTech services and ensure that companies provide clear, accurate, and transparent information about their products.

Building Trust Through Education

Educated consumers are likely to have more trust in FinTech services. Understanding how these services work, the security measures in place, and their rights as consumers can build confidence in using FinTech solutions.

Ongoing Education and Adaptation

Financial education is not a one-time effort but an ongoing process. As FinTech evolves, so too should educational programs, ensuring that consumers stay informed about new technologies, services, and potential risks.

Financial literacy and consumer education are foundational to the sustainable growth of the FinTech sector. By empowering consumers with the knowledge and skills to use FinTech services effectively and safely, we can enhance their financial well-being and ensure the continued development of a robust and inclusive financial ecosystem. This chapter highlights the importance of these aspects, outlining the steps needed to integrate financial literacy into the fabric of FinTech innovation and adoption.

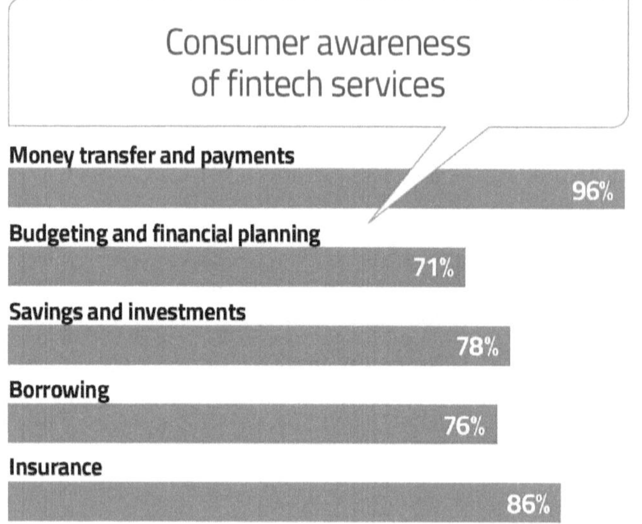

Financial Literacy and Consumer Education

"India's FinTech revolution is not just about finance;
it's about building a future where everyone has a
chance to prosper."

৫৩

XVIII

The Rural Reach: FinTech in India's Countryside

Discussing the Expansion and Impact of FinTech in Rural Areas

In a country as diverse and vast as India, the reach of financial technology (FinTech) in rural areas is a critical aspect of its overall success and impact. This chapter explores how FinTech is expanding into India's countryside, examining its influence on rural economies and communities.

Bridging the Urban-Rural Divide

Historically, rural areas in India have had limited access to traditional banking and financial services. FinTech presents an opportunity to bridge this urban-rural divide

by providing accessible, affordable, and convenient financial services to remote and underserved communities.

The Role of Mobile Technology

The widespread adoption of mobile phones in rural India has been a key driver in the expansion of FinTech services. Mobile-based FinTech solutions, including payments, banking, and insurance, are becoming increasingly accessible in rural areas, facilitating transactions and financial inclusion.

Overcoming Connectivity and Literacy Challenges

One of the primary challenges in rural FinTech adoption is the variability in internet connectivity and digital literacy. Initiatives aimed at enhancing digital infrastructure and providing basic digital literacy training are essential for the effective use of FinTech services in these areas.

Impact on Agricultural Sector

FinTech has a significant impact on the agricultural sector, which is the backbone of rural economies. Digital lending platforms and insurance products tailored for farmers can provide much-needed financial support, mitigating risks and contributing to increased productivity and income.

Microfinance and Peer-to-Peer Lending

Microfinance institutions and peer-to-peer lending platforms, facilitated by FinTech, play a crucial role in providing credit to rural entrepreneurs and small businesses. These services help in catalyzing economic activities and fostering entrepreneurship in rural areas.

Financial Inclusion and Empowerment

FinTech services contribute to financial inclusion by offering rural populations access to banking services, savings accounts, and affordable credit options. This inclusion promotes economic empowerment, helping individuals and communities to break out of poverty cycles.

Challenges in Deployment

Deploying FinTech solutions in rural areas comes with its own set of challenges, including ensuring the adaptability of services to local needs, addressing language barriers, and building trust among rural consumers who may be wary of digital financial services.

Government Initiatives and Policies

The Indian government's initiatives, such as the Jan Dhan Yojana and Digital India, play a significant role in promoting the use of FinTech in rural areas. Policies that encourage the development of rural-focused FinTech services can further accelerate this trend.

The Way Forward

For FinTech to fully realize its potential in rural India, continued innovation tailored to rural needs, along with ongoing investment in digital infrastructure and literacy, is crucial. Collaboration between FinTech companies, government agencies, and local communities is key to designing and implementing effective solutions.

The expansion of FinTech into rural India holds immense promise for socio-economic development. By providing access to financial services, FinTech can play a transformative role in the lives of millions in India's countryside, driving financial inclusion, and empowering rural communities. This chapter underscores the importance of extending the reach of FinTech beyond urban centers, highlighting both the opportunities and challenges in bridging the rural-urban financial divide.

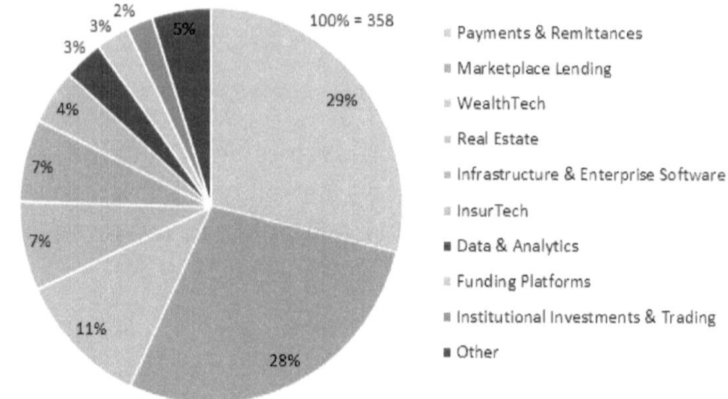

Source: FinTech Global

The Rural Reach

ॐ

"The true success of India's FinTech revolution lies in bridging the gap between the haves and the have-nots."

౮

XIX
Sustainable FinTech: Aligning with Environmental Goals

Exploring the Role of FinTech in Promoting Sustainable Finance

As global awareness of environmental issues grows, the financial sector is increasingly recognizing the importance of sustainability. This chapter explores how FinTech is contributing to this shift towards sustainable finance, aligning financial activities with broader environmental and social goals.

The Concept of Sustainable FinTech

Sustainable FinTech refers to the integration of innovative financial technologies with sustainable development principles. It encompasses a range of practices and products that aim to address environmental challenges, promote social development, and deliver financial returns.

Green Digital Payments

One of the primary contributions of FinTech to sustainability is the promotion of digital, paperless transactions. By reducing the reliance on physical cash and paper-based systems, FinTech helps in lowering the carbon footprint associated with traditional banking activities.

Impact Investing Platforms

FinTech has enabled the growth of impact investing platforms which allow individuals and institutions to invest in projects and businesses that generate measurable social and environmental impact alongside financial returns. These platforms make it easier for investors to contribute to sustainable development goals.

Blockchain for Transparency and Accountability

Blockchain technology is being leveraged to enhance transparency and accountability in sustainable finance. It can track the flow of funds and ensure that they are used for their intended sustainable purposes, thereby increasing investor confidence.

Crowdfunding for Green Projects

Crowdfunding platforms have become a popular tool for raising funds for environmentally-focused projects. These platforms allow individuals to directly fund renewable energy projects, conservation efforts, and other green initiatives.

Carbon Credit Trading and FinTech

FinTech is playing a role in the carbon credit market by facilitating the trading of carbon credits. This not only helps in the efficient functioning of the carbon market but also encourages companies to reduce their carbon emissions.

ESG (Environmental, Social, and Governance) Analytics

FinTech companies are developing sophisticated tools for ESG analytics. These tools help investors assess the sustainability performance of companies and guide investment decisions towards more environmentally and socially responsible businesses.

Challenges and Opportunities

While Sustainable FinTech holds great promise, it faces challenges such as the need for

standardization in sustainability metrics and ensuring the accessibility of sustainable financial products to a broader audience. Overcoming these challenges requires collaborative efforts among FinTech companies, regulatory bodies, and environmental experts.

Regulatory Frameworks and Incentives

The development of regulatory frameworks and incentives that support sustainable practices in the financial sector is crucial. Governments and international bodies can play a significant role in fostering a conducive environment for sustainable FinTech.

Education and Awareness

Raising awareness about the importance of sustainable finance and educating consumers and investors about sustainable FinTech options are vital for driving adoption. Increased awareness can lead to greater demand for sustainable financial products and services.

The Future of Sustainable FinTech

Looking forward, Sustainable FinTech is expected to grow and evolve, driven by increasing environmental concerns, consumer demand, and regulatory changes. Innovations in this space are likely to continue, offering new ways to align financial activities with environmental sustainability.

Sustainable FinTech represents a convergence of financial innovation and environmental consciousness. It offers a pathway to align financial services with the urgent need for environmental sustainability, enabling finance to be a force for good in addressing global challenges. This chapter highlights the role of FinTech in promoting sustainable finance, exploring the opportunities and challenges in this emerging field and its potential to contribute to a more sustainable and equitable future.

Sustainable FinTech

"In the algorithm of India's progress, FinTech is the most exciting variable."

৪৩

XX

Global Comparison: India's FinTech Scene in the World Arena

Comparing India's FinTech Ecosystem with Global Trends and Developments

As the FinTech sector continues to flourish worldwide, it's insightful to position India's FinTech ecosystem within the global context. This chapter explores how India's FinTech scene compares with global trends, identifying unique characteristics, strengths, and areas for growth.

India's Unique FinTech Landscape

India's FinTech landscape is unique, shaped by its vast population, diverse economy, and specific regulatory environment. Factors like a large unbanked population, high mobile phone penetration, and progressive government policies

have played crucial roles in shaping India's FinTech narrative. This contrasts with more mature FinTech markets like the UK or the US, where FinTech growth has been driven largely by innovation in financial services for already banked populations.

Government Initiatives and Regulatory Environment

India's approach to regulation has been a key differentiator. Initiatives like Aadhaar, the world's largest biometric ID system, and the Unified Payments Interface (UPI) system have provided a robust foundation for FinTech growth, unlike anything seen in most other countries. This government-backed infrastructure has been pivotal in promoting financial inclusion and digital payments at a massive scale.

Focus on Financial Inclusion

India's FinTech ecosystem has a strong focus on financial inclusion, catering to a large segment of the population

that was previously underserved by traditional banking systems. This contrasts with many Western countries, where FinTech developments often target the already banked population with more sophisticated financial products and services.

The Digital Payments Revolution

India's digital payments sector, particularly post-demonetization and with the advent of UPI, has seen explosive growth, setting it apart from many other countries. This rapid adoption of digital payments has been facilitated by a regulatory environment conducive to innovation and collaboration between the government and private sector.

The Role of Startups and Innovation

The Indian FinTech scene is characterized by a vibrant startup culture, driven by innovation and entrepreneurship. This has led to a proliferation of FinTech startups across various segments, including payments, lending, insurance (InsurTech), and wealth management (WealthTech). In contrast, in some developed markets, FinTech growth is often led by existing financial institutions adopting new technologies.

Scaling and Global Expansion

While Indian FinTech firms have successfully addressed local needs, scaling globally has been a challenge compared to FinTechs in regions like Europe and North America, where companies often expand internationally early in their lifecycle.

Collaborations and Partnerships

India has seen significant collaboration between FinTech startups and traditional financial institutions, a trend that is also observed globally. However, the nature and extent of these collaborations can vary, influenced by factors like market maturity, regulatory environments, and technological infrastructure.

Challenges and Opportunities

India faces unique challenges like financial literacy, regional diversity, and infrastructural constraints, which influence the FinTech ecosystem differently compared to other regions. However, these challenges also present opportunities for innovative solutions tailored to the local context.

India's FinTech ecosystem, while sharing some global trends, has distinct characteristics shaped by its unique challenges and opportunities. Its journey offers valuable insights into how FinTech can drive financial inclusion and innovation in a diverse and rapidly developing economy. This chapter not only positions India's FinTech scene within the global arena but also underscores its potential to influence global FinTech trends and serve as a model for other emerging economies.

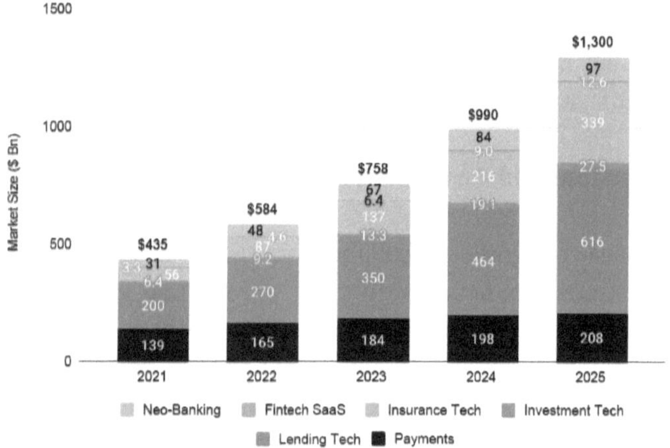

Global Comparison

☙

"India's FinTech: Where challenges are the crucible for innovation, and opportunities are the reward."

༓

XXI

The Road Ahead: Future Trends and Predictions in Indian FinTech

Speculating on Future Developments and Potential of FinTech in India

As the FinTech landscape in India continues to evolve at a rapid pace, this chapter explores the potential future trends and developments in this dynamic sector. It offers a speculative look into what the future may hold for Indian FinTech, considering current trajectories and emerging technologies.

Enhanced Integration of AI and Machine Learning

The future of Indian FinTech is likely to see a deeper integration of Artificial Intelligence (AI) and Machine Learning (ML). These technologies could revolutionize everything from personalized banking experiences and customer service (through chatbots and

AI-driven advisors) to more sophisticated risk assessment and fraud detection mechanisms.

Expansion of Blockchain Applications

Blockchain technology holds significant promise beyond cryptocurrencies. Its potential for creating secure, transparent, and efficient systems could see broader applications in areas like remittances, contract management, and secure document verification, potentially transforming the traditional banking infrastructure.

Growth of Neobanks

Neobanks, or digital-only banks, are expected to grow in number and scale, offering more comprehensive banking services and competing more directly with traditional banks. Their agility, innovative services, and customer-centric models could see them gaining a larger market share.

Financial Inclusion Through FinTech

One of the most significant impacts of FinTech in the future could be in driving financial inclusion. Leveraging technology to reach the unbanked and underbanked populations of India will remain a key focus, potentially transforming the socio-economic landscape of the country.

Emergence of RegTech

Regulatory Technology (RegTech) is set to become more prominent as FinTech companies and traditional financial institutions grapple with the growing complexity of regulatory compliance. RegTech can offer efficient solutions to manage compliance and reporting, reducing costs and improving accuracy.

Rise of InsurTech and WealthTech

InsurTech (insurance technology) and WealthTech (wealth management technology) are expected to see significant advancements, offering more personalized, accessible, and cost-effective solutions in insurance and wealth management.

Cross-Border Payments and Global Integration

Enhancements in FinTech may facilitate smoother cross-border transactions, overcoming current barriers in international payments. This could lead to better integration of the Indian FinTech ecosystem with global financial networks.

Focus on Cybersecurity

As FinTech continues to grow, so will the focus on cybersecurity. Protecting sensitive financial data against increasingly sophisticated cyber threats will be paramount, with FinTech firms likely investing heavily in advanced security technologies.

Sustainable and Socially Responsible FinTech

Sustainable FinTech solutions that align with environmental and social governance (ESG) goals could see increased focus. This trend would align with global movements towards sustainable and ethical financing.

The future of FinTech in India is poised at an exciting juncture, with the potential to redefine the financial landscape of the country. The trends and developments speculated in this chapter suggest a trajectory towards more inclusive, efficient, and innovative financial services. As technology continues to evolve and integrate into the financial sector, the potential for transformative change is immense. The road ahead for Indian FinTech is not just about technological advancements but also about harnessing these innovations to foster economic growth, financial inclusion, and sustainable development.

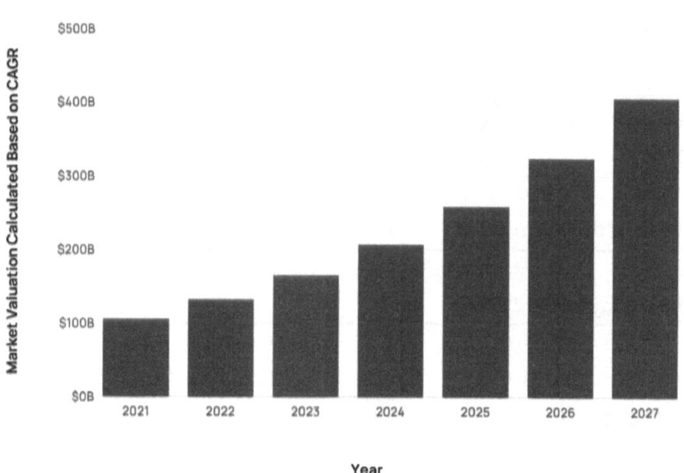

Future Trends and Predictions in Indian FinTech

"Through FinTech, India is not just connecting dots between people and finance; it's creating a constellation of opportunities."

౮౦

CITATION AND REFERENCE

This book has been written after extensive research and analysis, which involved referencing various books, as well as the author's study and practical experiences. The author has also searched various websites to gather valuable information and data about FinTech Revolution in India.

The author has taken great care to ensure that all information presented is accurate and properly cited to give credit to the sources. However, despite our best efforts, human errors may still occur. If any reader discovers any errors in this book, the author respectfully welcomes their feedback and encourages them to bring it to our attention.

Such feedback is valuable, and the author will take all necessary steps to correct any errors and improve the content of this book in future editions. Thank you for your understanding and support in this regard.

The author respects the right to freedom of speech and expression guaranteed by Article 19(1)(a) of the Constitution of India."

CONTACT

Jaiswal Brajesh & Co.
Chartered Accountants
15, Siddharth Complex, Mahmoorganj Road,
Sigra, Varanasi (U.P.) 221010
email: brajeshindiag20@gmail.com

|| LOKAHA SAMASTHAHA SUKHINO BHAVANTU ||

www.ingramcontent.com/pod-product-compliance
Lightning Source LLC
Chambersburg PA
CBHW020543160726
47991CB00002B/568